B.S.U.C. - LIBRARY

00204017

D0312061

# WHO AM I?

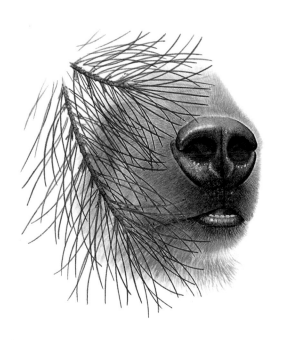

I am brown and furry, strong and scary.
I live in the woods.

# WHO AM I?

By Moira Butterfield
Illustrated by Wayne Ford

Belitha Press

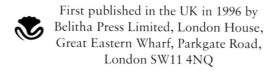

First published in the UK in 1996 by
Belitha Press Limited, London House,
Great Eastern Wharf, Parkgate Road,
London SW11 4NQ

Copyright © in this format Belitha Press Limited 1996

All rights reserved. No part of this book may be reproduced or
utilized in any form or by any means, electronic or mechanical,
including photocopying, recording or by any information storage and
retrieval system, without permission in writing from the publisher,
except by a reviewer who may quote brief passages in a review.

ISBN 1 85561 575 4

British Library in Cataloguing in Publication Data for this book
is available from the British Library.

Printed in Portugal

Editor: Stephanie Bellwood
Designer: Helen James
Illustrator: Wayne Ford / Wildlife Art Agency
Consultant: Andrew Branson

BATH SPA UNIVERSITY
COLLEGE
NEWTON PARK LIBRARY

Class No.
JF4 BUT

Res      16. MAR. 1999

DISCARD

My fur is soft. My nose is long.
My claws are sharp.
My paws are strong.
Around the forest paths I prowl...
Be careful not to make me growl.

Who am I?

# Here is my fur

It is brown and
soft and grows
all over my body.
Can you see my
round furry ears
sticking up?

The weather is
often cold and
snowy where
I live. My thick
fur coat keeps
me warm.

# Here are my teeth

I use them to eat lots of different things. I like to munch fat juicy blackberries.

I like to eat honey too. Sometimes I follow bees to find their nest full of sweet honey.

# Here is my paw

I have long sharp claws to dig up tasty roots and little animals from under the ground.

Sometimes I stand in the river to catch food. Can you see what I am holding in my paw?

# Here is my nose

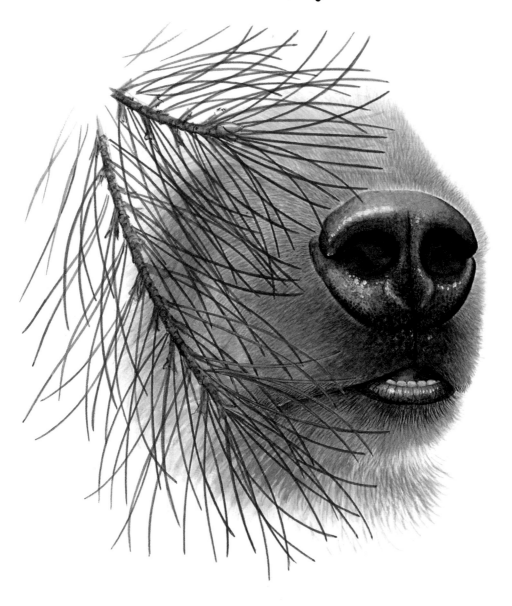

It is called my
snout. I can smell
food from far away.
There is no food
at this camp site.

The campers hang
their food in a bag
between two trees.
I can smell the food
but I can't reach it.

# Here is my eye

I can't see very far.
Can you see the deer
standing on the hill?
I can't see her but
I can smell her.

In winter I hide
in my home.
I shut my eyes
and sleep for
weeks and weeks
until it is spring.

# Here are my legs

I stand on my back legs to scratch a tree with my claws. Then I leave my smell on it.

Other animals like me see the scratches and smell the tree. They know I live nearby.

# Here is my home

It is called a den. It may be a cave or a hole I have dug in the ground. I sleep safe and sound inside. If I am woken up it makes me angry.

I open my mouth and...
# growl!

Have you guessed who I am?

# I am a bear

Point to my ...

round ears

long nose

furry tail

brown eyes

strong paws

sharp claws

I am called
a brown bear.

# Here are my babies

They are called cubs. When they are born they are tiny. They stay in the den with me.

When they grow bigger they go out to play. They chase each other and climb trees.

This is where I live

I live in a wood.

Can you see a deer, two chipmunks,
a bees' nest and a woodpecker?

# Here is a map of the world

I live in lots of
different countries.
Can you see some
of the places where
I live?

Can you point to the
place where you live?

North
America

The places where
I live are this colour.

Russia

Europe

# Can you answer these questions about me?

What colour is my fur?

Do I like to eat berries?

What else do I like to eat?

Can I smell things that are far away?

Can I see a long way?

What are my babies called?

What do I use my claws for?

What is my home called?

How do I spend the winter?

# Here are some words to learn about me

**claws** The long sharp nails on my paws. I have five claws on each paw.

**den** My hidden home in a cave or a hole that I have dug in the ground.

**fur** My warm soft coat. It is very thick and it keeps me warm.

**growl** The noise I make when I am angry. Can you make a growling noise like me?

**munch**  The way I chew my food.

**paws**  My furry hands and feet. I can catch fish with my paws.

**prowl**  The slow and careful way I move when I am looking for food.

**roots**  The parts of a plant that grow in the ground. I like to dig them up and eat them.

**snout**  My long nose.

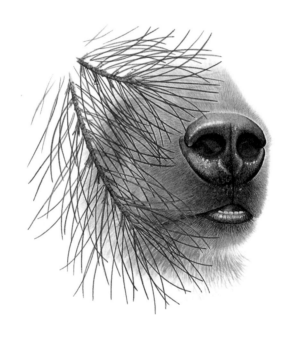